UNTOLD THOUGHTS

Ubah Hussien

BookLeaf Publishing
India | USA | UK

Untold thoughts

© 2021 Ubah Hussien

All rights reserved.

Presentation by *BookLeaf Publishing*

Web: www.bookleafpub.com

E-mail: info@bookleafpub.com

ISBN: 9789358360936

First edition 2021

1

The world is a garden

Our world is a garden that is full of twisted leaves and

dead plants

A garden that has not been planted for a long time

Full of unfinished knots that is yet to be untied

A garden whose owners disappeared What happened to

the garden?

The beauty of the garden lies beyond what meets the

eye

A garden is what we imagine it to be

A garden is full of fresh flowers with bells around the

bushes

Each plant is alive and well fed

The garden is vibrant and full of colours

The world is a garden

Plant it with every seed you have

2

The lost Princess of the land

This lost princess has lost her way through swimming

with sea monsters

sea monsters disguised as mermaids

mermaids who love all things humans

She was craving love and friendship Something she was

starving on land

The Princess was feeling blue

Teased and alone

How much can one take?

The Princess had enough and set herself free

The soft sand is where she is at

Ready to jump into the sea she craved

Filled with such wonderful things

Seahorses

Goldfish

You name it

The Princess felt welcomed

She arrived at a huge castle

One filled with sea shells and pebbles

She knocked on the door

A beautiful mermaid appears

The Princess stunned at his physical appearance His

upper body strength greatly impressed her

Talk after talk

A friendship was born

The trust grew So did the secrets she told him

The Princess was no longer alone

She found her calling

In a form of a mermaid

The mermaid wanted to ask what the Land is like

She talks of bad memories and secrets

They talk

They laugh

The Princess felt loved by this new dream of hers

But the dream became a nightmare

Yet she did not know

The mermaid and the Princess stood outside

He took her hand

They Swam where the dolphins were

Swam past the sea horses

Swam straight through the goldfish The mermaid and

the Princess met his friends

They talked

They swam Finally The Princess was tired

"I need to rest" "I need to rest"

The Mermaid took her to a cave

Filled with sharks and other dangerous creatures

The mermaids took the Princess inside and laughed

Laughed as they took her voice away

Laughed as they tortured her

Laughed as The Princess succumbed

The lost Princess lost her way by swimming with sea

monsters

Sea monsters disguised as beautiful mermaids

The Princess who was once on land

Is now laying down on the sea No one knows where she

is

No one ever saw her again.

3

Hope

In dark days like these

we are frightened of what life has become

our fears are now in front of us

left right and centre "the end is here" they say all hope

is lost

or so we think

A shining light awaits us from afar

Though we are unaware

What the future would be

Our hearts and minds are bursting with with fear and

hope

The two words that cannot be mates

One is a enemy and one is a friend

We must decide our fate

Fear was a cruel person

Always letting our feelings down

But hope is the friend we need when we need cheering

up

Hope will save us from the horrible fear

Hope is like a songbird It will fill your soul with the

beautiful tune and melodies

It will make you feel warm And refreshes your soul.

In dark days like these, hope is your only friend

An invisible guardian angel

We can't seem them but we can feel their presence In

our heart and soul

4

The first time

The first time we met

We were young

Innocent

Carefree

The first time we met

We were joyous and no hard feelings

Our childhood was heavenly as

We walked without running

The first time we met

Our smiles were equal

We were equal

We closed our eyes and imagined We would stay

together

Now

We are nothing like before

We don't speak of each other

For there have been Destruction The music does not fit

in with us no more

No rhythm ,no beat All gone

We were gone

The silence was unbearable

It ached

We find ourselves getting smaller and smaller

We could not see each other no more

The first time we met

We were over the moon

Little did we know

It would end in destruction and despair

5

I ,Seizure

Few minutes a night

I drop to the ground

I say 'Hello darkness it's me again'

I no longer have control over my body

Twitches and turns take over

I cannot feel what's around me

For I have no control over my seizures

I am inside a dark hole waiting to be let out

I don't know how, I don't know when

There is no sign

I have no memory of coming into the dark hole and I

have no memory of coming out

I wake up in broad daylight In the hospital Where I lay

down and wondering What will become of me

6

Dear life

 I always wondered Is life a dream or a nightmare?

For some a dream

Some a nightmare

Sometimes there are rays of sunshine and happiness

At times clouds of sadness

With each passing day there is a new problem and a
new solution

Why is it so complicated? And what's the answer?

Life It's called life.

7

Ode to a lady's diary

Oh Sweet old diary,

You never fail to listen to my worries

You are always there for me whenever I am sad or

happy You have melted me with love and patience

You are a friend with care With your beautiful soft

paper to pour my soul

Our secret chats Do you remember?

It was you and me against the world

And I love you for it

Thank you so much

For being a friend I can write to.

8

Numb

I feel safe from being hurt

I no longer experience pains A comfort that is strange

But satisfying Without people

I don't feel disappointed

9

Hidden pain

I tell myself keep your sad feelings hidden They will go

away soon

And happiness will take over

But sadness takes over too

I smile to keep people from telling me to smile

But I don't want to I don't feel like smiling This hidden

pain I keep inside So others can sleep peacefully But

what about me?

I cannot keep this up no more

This hidden pain

Is keeping me hidden From loved ones

10

Yours truly, me

I don't follow your rules I'm not easy to deal with I

don't fit in a crowd But that's cool with me

You don't control me

My feelings

Or my life

I am not perfect But I'm not a puppet either

Yours truly

Me

11

Spring

Now winter has left

Daisies are opening

 With everything growing Leaves, flowers , roses

You can smell it arriving Hearing the morning chirp

from birds

The whole world is waking up to the sound of spring

Shiny upon us

The beautiful fields are full of hope

Let's run in meadows and feel the air

To celebrate life

And the return of spring

12

Someday

The most heartbreaking word is someday

You will someday make the team

You will someday get the job

You will someday have a happy ending When is it my

time to shine?

Someday

13

Summer breeze

Looking forward to the days

Where the sun is with me

Through the breezy winds

The sun is always there to shine It's golden round face

is what I see when I wake up

And what I feel when I'm sad

Now that the summer is out

I can spread my wings

 And go wherever the summer breeze takes me

14

Victory

 There is a war inside me that I'm not familiar with

Something so big I cannot handle I'm losing control of

everything The walls are cracking

What do I do?

There is victory ahead But I cannot see it

There is too much darkness in front of me

I need to find the switch to light up the room

The switch is getting closer

My hand is just waiting to switch the light on

Is this a sign?

Am I on the road to victory?

Only time will tell

Until then

I keep climbing

15

Blackout

I walk to the living room to grab something

Walking, walking

Suddenly I drop

I'm faced with a blackout

With no one to see

No one to go

No one to ask for help

Meanwhile my body is shaking

Shaking so hard

I can't feel it

I don't remember it

But folks told me

What I cannot feel

Or understand

Why is this blackout happening to me?

16

I fear

As I walk away

I hear something calling me

'I'll get you , I'll get you"

But I cannot see

Or touch it

I fear I am going crazy

I walk faster and fast

I keep hearing the same sound

Why am I hearing this?

Am I scared?

I don't know

But I will face it

Sooner or later

17

Heal

I cry a lot But I get it together

I turn sadness into kindness I search for love

But not disappointment

 I feed my soul with acceptance

By acceptance I heal myself

I heal for myself

And that's the way to go

18

Imagination

I lock myself inside my own mind

Living rent free with no noise

I let my imagination get the better of me

But I like it like that

Life outside is scary

I get sad and angry I scream with agony But I can't

express myself

With all my emotions I struggle to put words together

Only to be misunderstood

I lock myself in my imagination

It's much safer there

I can feel

I can express And most importantly

I am me

19

Imagination

I lock myself inside my own mind

Living rent free with no noise

I let my imagination get the better of me

But I like it like that

Life outside is scary

I get sad and angry I scream with agony But I can't

express myself

With all my emotions I struggle to put words together

Only to be misunderstood I lock myself in my

imagination It's much safer there

I can feel

I can express And most importantly

I am me

20

Eye of the beholder

Beauty is in the eye of the beholder they say

But what's in the eye?

Who is the beholder ?

We see what are minds want to see

Some see beauty in trees

Some see Beauty in clouds Others don't see beauty at all

But there is beauty around

One must find it closely

21

End

What is the end ?

Is it the end of a journey ?

Or simply the beginning of the rest of our lives

One would realise the end is near

When they are yearning for adventure

Yearning for change

The end is the beginning of a new chapter of our story

One where we are the writers

We decide what our story is

What is the end?

It's simple

It's the start of a new life

www.ingramcontent.com/pod-product-compliance
Lightning Source LLC
LaVergne TN
LVHW021344200726
843509LV00014B/2666